Your Body and You

YOU'RE UNIQUE

By Anita Ganeri   Illustrated by Vera Popova

PowerKiDS press

Published in 2025 by The Rosen Publishing Group, Inc.
2544 Clinton Street, Buffalo, NY 14224

Copyright © The Watts Publishing Group, 2021

All rights reserved. No part of this book may be reproduced
in any form without permission in writing from the publisher, except by a reviewer.

Credits
Series editor: Julia Bird
Illustrator: Vera Popova
Packaged by: Collaborate

Note to parents and teachers: every effort has been made by the Publishers to ensure websites are suitable for children, that they are of the highest educational value, and that they contain no inappropriate or offensive material. However, because of the nature of the Internet, it is impossible to guarantee that the contents of these sites will not be altered. We strongly advise that Internet access is supervised by a responsible adult.

Cataloging-in-Publication Data

Names: Ganeri, Anita, 1961-, author. | Popova, Vera, illustrator.
Title: You're unique / by Anita Ganeri, illustrated by Vera Popova.
Description: Buffalo, NY : Powerkids Press, 2025. | Series: Your body and you | Includes glossary and index.
Identifiers: ISBN 9781499445558 (pbk.) | ISBN 9781499445565 (library bound) | ISBN 9781499445572 (ebook)
Subjects: LCSH: Individuality--Juvenile literature. | Individuality in children--Juvenile literature. | Individual differences--Juvenile literature. | Children--Conduct of life--Juvenile literature.
Classification: LCC BF723.I56 G326 2025 | DDC 155.2--dc23

Manufactured in the United States of America
CPSIA Compliance Information: Batch #CSPK25. For further information contact Rosen Publishing at 1-800-237-9932.

CONTENTS

Who are you? 4
Unique you 6
Brilliant bodies 8
Becoming you 10
Brown eyes, blue eyes 12
Colors and curls 14
Skin deep 16
Brain power 18
Who am I? 20
Body image 22
Happy being me 24
Different, but the same 26
Be yourself 28
Glossary 30
Find out more 31
Index 32

WHO ARE YOU?

Have a look at yourself in the mirror. Look closely. What do you see?

Are you a boy or a girl? Are you tall or short? What color are your eyes? Is your hair curly or straight? Do you wear glasses or braces?

UNIQUE YOU

Look carefully at this picture. Can you see anyone like you?

There might be someone who looks a bit similar. But no one is exactly the same (not even identical twins!).

Everyone is different. Nobody else looks, thinks, or sounds exactly like you. There's never been anyone like you in the world, and there'll never be another you. You are unique.

Being unique can sometimes be tricky. You might wish you were taller, or better at singing, or looked more like your friends. Everybody is different. But we're also alike in many ways. It's important to accept other people for who they are. It's also important to treat everyone with kindness and respect.

BRILLIANT BODIES

Human bodies come in different shapes and sizes. But most people's bodies share the same design and work in the same way.

Your body is designed for walking upright. A long chain of bones, called your spine, runs down your back. At the bottom of your spine are your legs. At the top is your head, with your two eyes, two ears, and nose. Being high up means they can sense the world around you.

A frame of more than 200 bones, called your skeleton, protects your insides. It works with your muscles to help you to move. It also keeps your body in shape.

Spine

Skeleton

Without your skeleton, your body would collapse in a heap!

Muscles

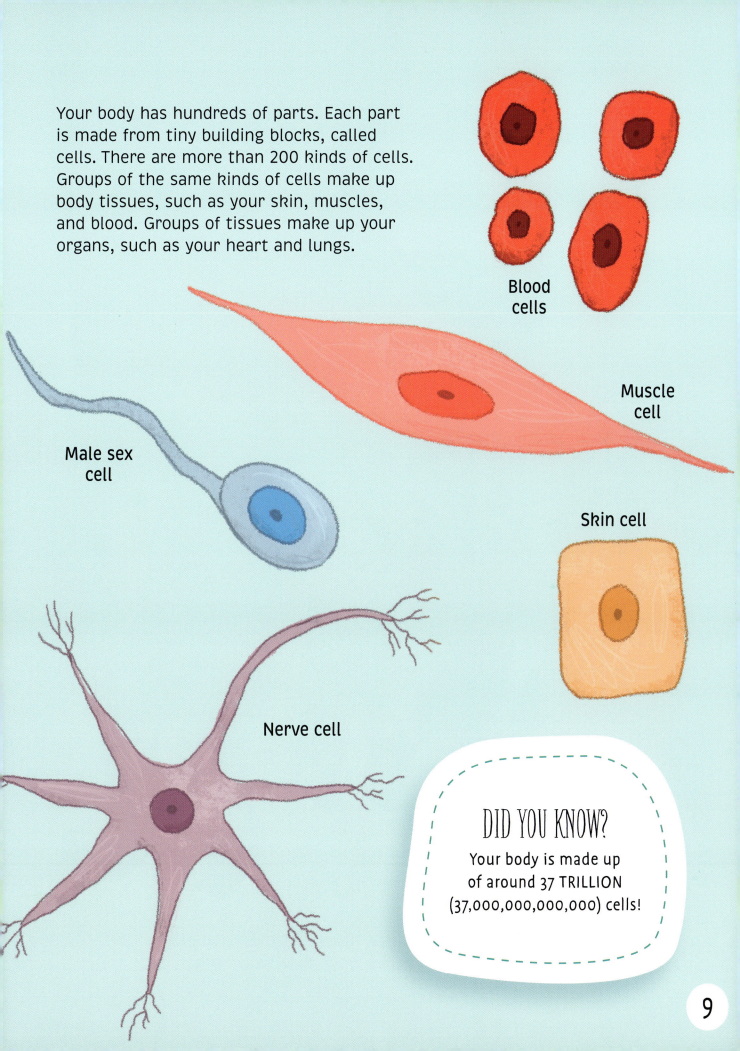

Your body has hundreds of parts. Each part is made from tiny building blocks, called cells. There are more than 200 kinds of cells. Groups of the same kinds of cells make up body tissues, such as your skin, muscles, and blood. Groups of tissues make up your organs, such as your heart and lungs.

Blood cells

Muscle cell

Male sex cell

Skin cell

Nerve cell

DID YOU KNOW?
Your body is made up of around 37 TRILLION (37,000,000,000,000) cells!

BECOMING YOU

The shape of your face, the color of your hair, how tall you are, if you have dimples – these are some of the things that make you unique. But why do you look like you?

Inside your cells are tiny threads, called chromosomes. They carry information called genes. Genes build your unique body. They help it to work properly and stay healthy. They decide your features and what you look like.

You get half of your genes from your mom and half from your dad. These genes work together. That's why you might look a bit like each of your parents.

Even so, you don't look exactly like your parents, or your brothers and sisters. This is because everyone, even identical twins, has a slightly different mix of genes.

BROWN EYES, BLUE EYES

Are your eyes brown or blue, or green, gray, or hazel?

The color in your eyes comes from a dark coloring, called melanin.

The more melanin in your eyes, the darker they are. Brown eyes contain lots of melanin. Blue eyes contain very little.

DID YOU KNOW?
Most people in the world have brown eyes. The rarest eye color is green.

You get your eye color from your parents. If you inherit two brown eye genes, your eyes will be brown. But what if you inherit one blue eye gene and one brown eye gene? What color will your eyes be? The answer is ... brown! This is because the brown eye gene is stronger than the blue eye one.

COLORS AND CURLS

Like the color of your eyes, your hair color comes from melanin.

The more melanin in your hair, the darker it is.

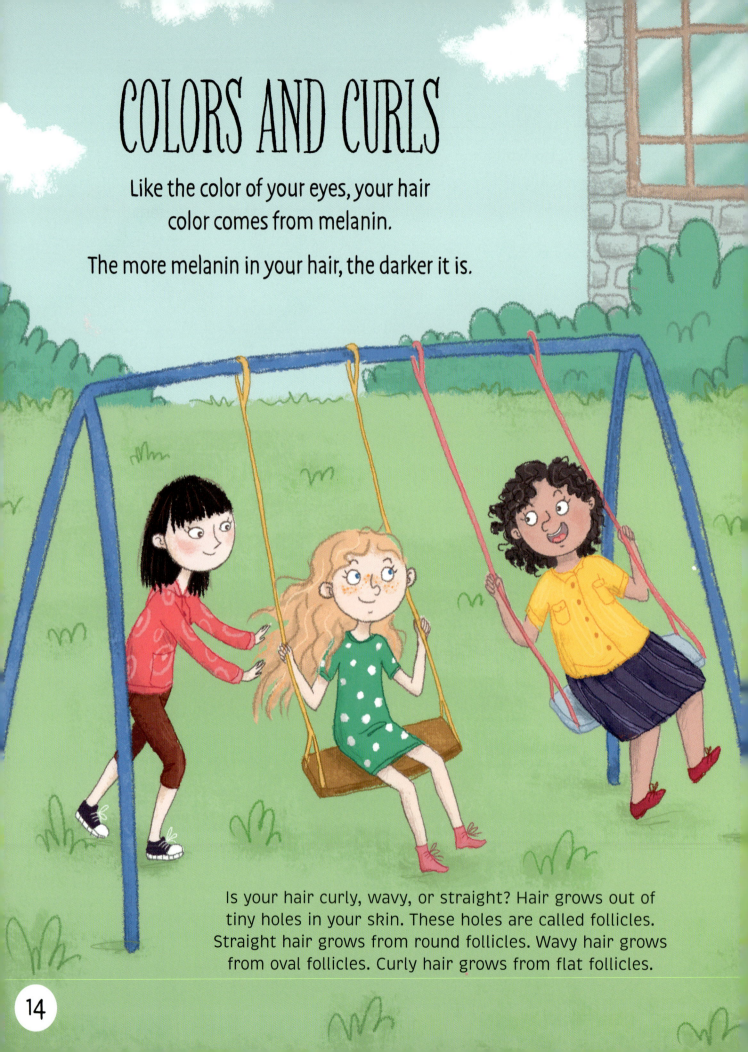

Is your hair curly, wavy, or straight? Hair grows out of tiny holes in your skin. These holes are called follicles. Straight hair grows from round follicles. Wavy hair grows from oval follicles. Curly hair grows from flat follicles.

You inherit curly, straight, or wavy hair from your parents. You also inherit your hair color. If you inherit one brown hair gene and one fair hair gene, your hair will be brown. This is because the brown hair gene is stronger.

Black and brown are the most common hair colors. Red is the rarest. To have red hair, you must inherit two red hair genes, one from each of your parents (though they won't necessarily have red hair themselves).

SKIN DEEP

Skin can be different colors, from dark brown to pale.

Like your eyes and hair, skin color comes from melanin. You inherit the color of your skin from your parents.

Melanin works like a natural sunscreen. It helps protect your skin from the sun's harmful ultraviolet (UV) rays. These can cause sunburn and even skin cancer. Dark skin contains more melanin than light skin. This means that dark skin has better protection against the sun.

Look at your fingertips. Can you see patterns in the skin? These are your fingerprints. They help your fingers grip and touch. No two people have the same fingerprints. This makes fingerprints very useful for identifying who you are.

DID YOU KNOW?
Humans aren't the only animals with fingerprints. Chimpanzees, gorillas, and koalas have them too.

Human

Gorilla

BRAIN POWER

Your brain controls your body, and everything you do.

Different parts of your brain have different jobs.

Moving, breathing, seeing, speaking, and remembering are just some of the things your brain controls. These are some of the things that make you you.

Your brain is kept busy. It sorts and stores messages from your body. Then it decides what action to take, and sends instructions to your body. These messages travel to and from your brain along wirelike cells, called nerves.

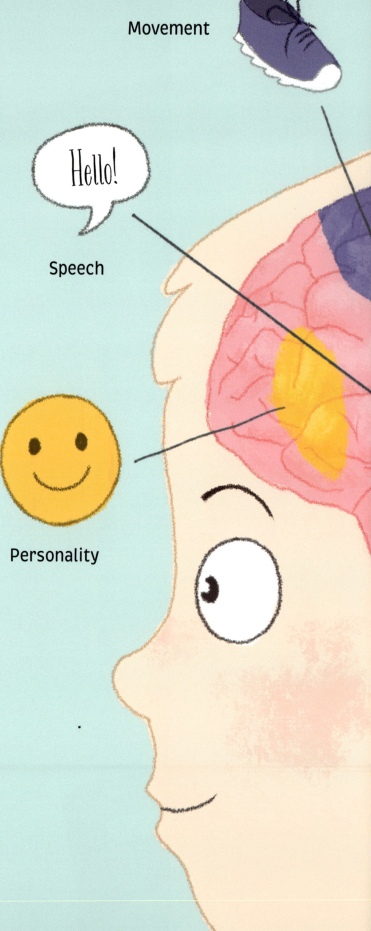

Movement

Speech

Personality

DID YOU KNOW?
Your brain is made up of billions of nerve cells. Each nerve cell is linked to thousands of others for sending messages.

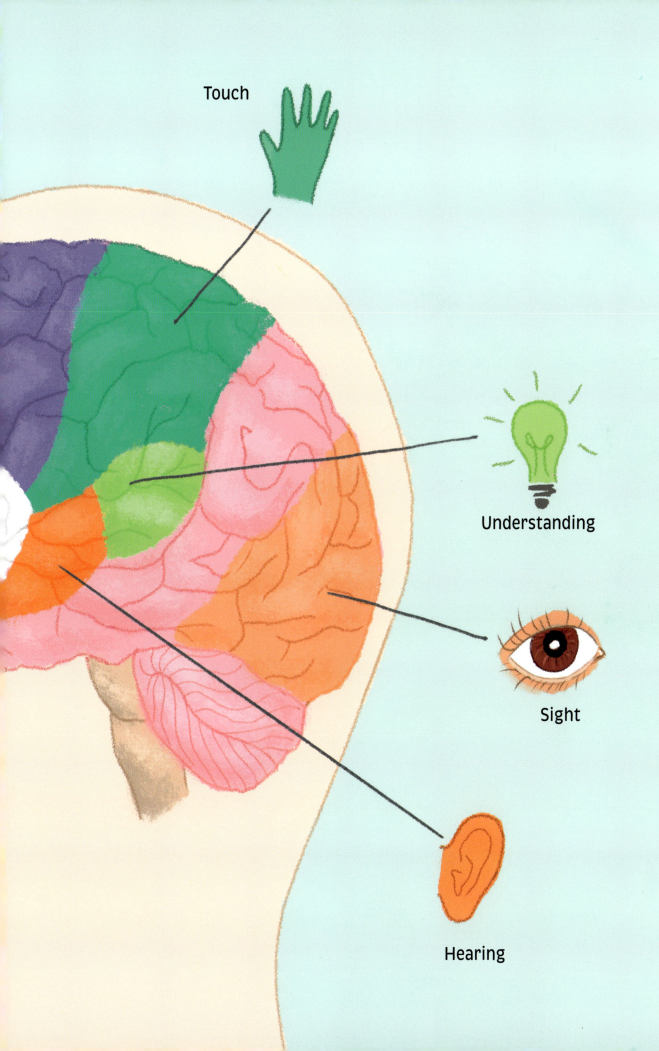

WHO AM I?

Most people's brains work in the same way. We all think, learn, and feel things, but everyone does these things in their own way.

Do you like the same things as your friends? What makes you happy or sad? Are you learning to play a musical instrument? Do you have a good sense of humor? Things like these help to make up your personality.

You inherit parts of your personality from your parents. If your mom or dad is good at art, you might be good at it too. But that's not all. As you grow up, you learn other skills, and things happen to you. You might get a pet, move to a new place, or go on a trip. All these experiences, and how they make you feel or behave, help to make you unique.

BODY IMAGE

Everybody's body is different. No two bodies are exactly the same shape and size.

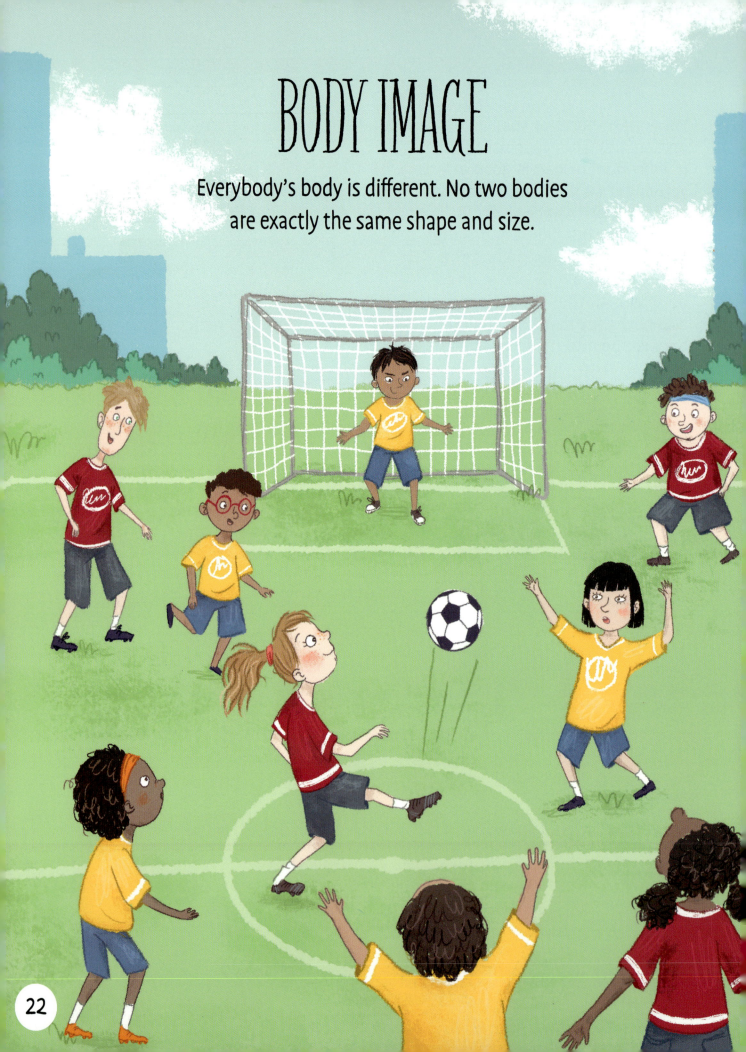

Sometimes, you might feel unhappy with how you look. You might wish you had curly hair like your best friend. You might wish you had green eyes. You might wear glasses or braces, and wish you didn't have to.

How you think and feel about your body is called body image. It's easy to pick out things you don't like about how you look, but it's much better to focus on the things you do like.

You might think you'd be more popular if you looked different. Most likely, your friends are thinking the same thing about themselves! You don't need to change anything to fit in – just be yourself. Remember, your friends like you for who you are.

HAPPY BEING ME

Being happy with how you look and who you are will make you more confident.

This can all take time. But there are lots of things you can try to look more confident, even if you're feeling like *wobbly jelly* inside.

Take a deep breath, and stand up tall. Put your shoulders back. You will immediately look more confident. At first, it may feel odd. Keep practicing, and it'll soon come naturally.

Speak to someone at school you haven't spoken to before. This can be scary if you're usually shy. Look them in the eye. Don't keep looking down or away from them.

DIFFERENT, BUT THE SAME

Being yourself is something to be proud of.

It's never okay for anyone to tease you or make you feel bad about how you look, what you wear, or how you speak. If this happens, it's important to tell your parents, a teacher, or another adult you trust. And it's never okay for you to treat anyone else badly because they don't look like you.

BE YOURSELF

Have another look at yourself in the mirror. Look closely. What do you see?

Is your list the same as it was at the start of this book?

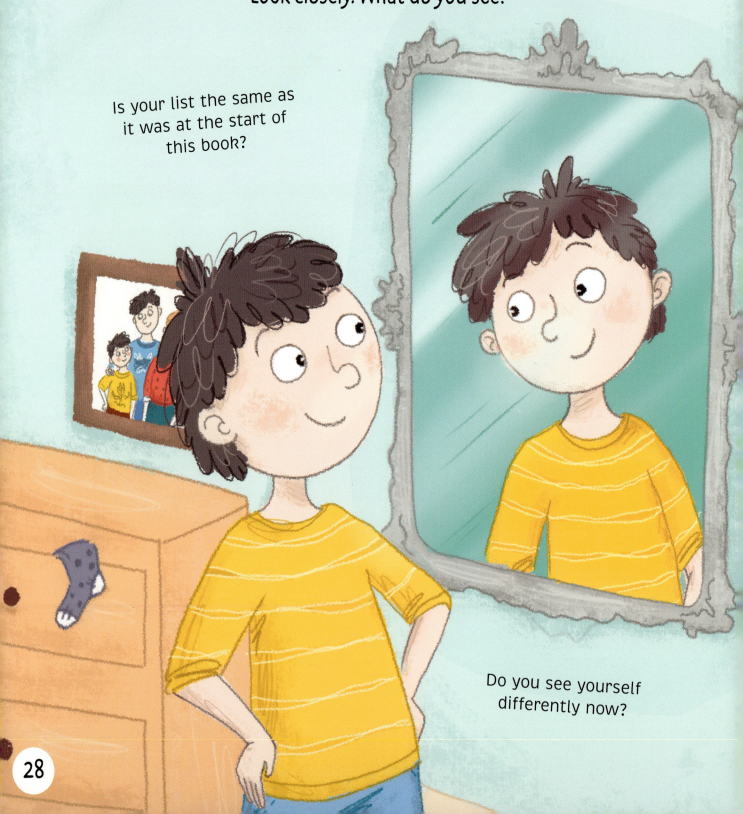

Do you see yourself differently now?

It's not always easy being unique when you just want to be the same as your friends. But now you know more about what makes you you. Hopefully, this will help you feel proud of who you are and more confident to be your unique self.

Being you, and being different, is fantastic. After all, think how boring the world would be if everyone was exactly the same!

GLOSSARY

Braces
Set of wires fixed to a person's teeth to make them straighter.

Confident
Feeling happy with yourself and what you can do.

Dimples
Small hollows that appear on a person's face when they smile.

Experience
Something that happens to you and affects how you feel.

Faith
Another word for a religion that someone follows.

Hazel
Greenish-brown or yellowish-brown color.

Identical
Exactly the same, or very similar.

Identifying
Recognizing someone or something.

Inherit
To share a feature, such as your eye color, with your parents or grandparents.

Personality
The type of person you are, shown by how you think, feel, and behave.

Respect
To show politeness and care towards someone.

Similar
Looking or being almost, but not exactly, the same.

Unique
The only one of its kind.

FIND OUT MORE

Websites

www.bbc.co.uk/bitesize/clips/z3xb9qt

Facts, figures, and video clips about your amazing body, and how it works.

https://kidshealth.org/en/kids/self-esteem.html

This site features tips for building confidence and self-esteem.

https://www.pbs.org/video/heredity-who-are-you-c7ngrj/#:~:text=The%20passing%20down%20of%20traits,make%20us%20who%20we%20are.

This website from PBS explains heredity and how each of us is truly unique.

Books

Love Your Body: Your Body Can Do Amazing Things
Jessica Sanders & Carol Rossetti (White Lion Publishing, 2020)

12 Hacks to Boost Self-Esteem
Honor Head (Enslow Publishing, 2023)

INDEX

being kind 5, 7, 26–27

being respectful 7, 26–27

body image 7, 22–24, 28–29

body organs 9

body tissues 9

body types 8–9, 22–23

bones 8

braces 4, 23

brain 18–20

cells 9–10, 18

chromosomes 10

confidence 24–29

eye color 4, 12–14, 16, 23

feeling shy 5, 24–25

feelings 20, 24–26

fingerprints 17

follicles, hair 14

genes 10–11, 13, 15

genetic inheritance 10–11, 13, 15–16, 21

glasses 4, 23

hair 4, 10–11, 14–16, 23, 27

height 4, 7, 10

learning 18, 20–21

melanin 12, 14, 16

muscles 8–9

nerves 9, 18

personality 5, 18–21

senses 8, 17–19

skin 9, 14, 16–17

twins 6, 11

ultraviolet (UV) rays 16